WELCOME TO MANDARIN CHINESE

with SESAME STREET

J. P. PRESS

Lerner Publications ◆ Minneapolis

Dear Parents and Educators,

From its very beginning, *Sesame Street* has promoted mutual respect and cultural understanding by featuring a cast of diverse and lovable characters. *Welcome to Mandarin Chinese* introduces children to the wonderful, wide world we live in. In this book *Sesame Street* friends present handy and fun vocabulary in a language kids may not know. These words can help young readers welcome new friends. Have fun as you explore!

Sincerely,

The Editors at Sesame Workshop

Table of Contents

WELCOME!   4

WELCOME!

欢迎!

(Say huān yíng)

How to Speak Mandarin Chinese

Mandarin Chinese can be written in a special system called Pinyin. Most letters in Pinyin sound the same as if you were reading English, but a few of the letters have slightly different sounds. For example, if you see a *c*, make the *ts* sound. This is how you would say the English sounds in Pinyin:

c = ts   x = sh   e = uh   ui =way
q = ch   z = dz   u = oo   i =ee

This is Lily. She lives in China.

Hello.
你好.
nǐ hǎo

Pinyin also shows you what tones to use with special accents on letters:

ē = flat tone, a little higher than regular speech
é = rising tone (like when you ask a question)
ě = falling, then rising tone
è = falling tone

What is your name?
你叫什么名字?
nǐ jiào shén me míng zi

My name is . . .
我叫 . . .
wǒ jiào . . .

friendship
友谊
yǒu yì

Will you be my friend?
你愿意做我的朋友吗?
nǐ yuàn yì zuò wǒ de péng you ma

You're my best friend!

你是我最好的朋友！

family
家庭
jiā tíng

dad
爸爸
bà ba

This is my mom.
这是我的妈妈.

brother
兄弟
xiōng di

sister
姐妹
jiě mèi

grandma
奶奶
nǎi nai

grandpa
爷爷
yé ye

Thank you.
谢谢.
xiè xie

You are welcome.
不客气.
bú kè qi

Please.
请.
qǐng

I'm sorry.
对不起.
duì bù qǐ

lunch
午餐
wǔ cān

breakfast
早餐
zǎo cān

snack
零食
líng shí

dinner
晚餐
wǎn cān

I'm thirsty.
我渴了.
wǒ kě le

15

How are you?
你好吗？
nǐ hǎo ma

I'm fine, thank you.
我很好, 谢谢你.
wǒ hěn hǎo xiè xiè nǐ

I like you.
我喜欢你.
wǒ xǐ huan nǐ

happy
高兴
gāo xìng

sad
难过
nán guò

18

proud
骄傲
jiāo ào

excited
激动
jī dòng

19

dog
狗
gǒu

animals
动物
dòng wù

fish
鱼
yú

bird
鸟
niǎo

cat
猫
māo

20

Animals
are great!
动物们真是
太有趣了!

21

colors
颜色
yán sè

My favorite color is . . .
页我最喜欢的颜色是...
wǒ zuì xǐ huan de
yán sè shì . . .

red
红色
hóng sè

orange
橙色
chéng sè

yellow
黄色
huáng sè

green
绿色
lǜ sè

blue
蓝色
lán sè

purple
紫色
zǐ sè

Let's play!
我们一起玩吧!
wǒ men yì qǐ wán ba

toys
玩具
wán jù

What do you like to do?
你喜欢做什么?
nǐ xǐ huan zuò shén me

I like to jump.
我喜欢跳来跳去.

Goodbye.
再见
zài jiàn

See you soon!
回头见！
huí tóu jiàn

Count It!

1 one
—
yī

2 two
二
èr

3 three
三
sān

4 four 四 sì

5 five 五 wǔ

6 six 六 liù

7 seven 七 qī

8 eight 八 bā

9 nine 九 jiǔ

10 ten 十 shí

Oscar's Favorite Words

I love trash!
我爱垃圾!

messy
乱糟糟的
luàn zāo zāo de

trash can
垃圾桶
lā jī tǒng

grumpy
暴躁的
bào zào de

Further Information

McSween, Michele Wong. *My First Mandarin Words with Gordon & Li Li.* New York: Cartwheel, 2018.

Moon, Walt K. *Let's Explore China.* Minneapolis: Lerner Publications, 2017.

National Geographic Kids: China
https://kids.nationalgeographic.com/explore/countries/china/#china-dragon.jpg

Panda Tree: Mandarin Games
https://www.pandatree.com/games/mandarin

Sesame Street
https://www.sesamestreet.org

Lerner Publications Company
An imprint of Lerner Publishing Group, Inc.
241 First Avenue North
Minneapolis, MN 55401 USA

For reading levels and more information, look up this title at www.lernerbooks.com.

Main body text set in Mikado.
Typeface provided by HVD.

Additional image credits: ESB Professional/Shutterstock.com, p. 20 (dog); clarst5/Shutterstock.com, p. 20 (bird); Eric Isselee/Shutterstock.com, p. 20 (cat); Gunnar Pippel/Shutterstock.com, p. 20 (fish); Super Prin/Shutterstock.com, p. 23 (butterfly); kazoka/Shutterstock.com, pp. 28–29 (frog).

Library of Congress Cataloging-in-Publication Data

Names: Press, J. P., 1993– author. | Children's Television Workshop, contributor.
Title: Welcome to Mandarin Chinese with Sesame Street / J. P. Press.
Other titles: Sesame Street (Television program)
Description: Minneapolis : Lerner Publications, 2019. | Series: Sesame Street welcoming words | Includes bibliographical references.
Identifiers: LCCN 2018059334 (print) | LCCN 2019008436 (ebook) | ISBN 9781541562516 (eb pdf) | ISBN 9781541555037 (lb : alk. paper) | ISBN 9781541574960 (pb : alk. paper)
Subjects: LCSH: Chinese language—Conversation and phrase books—English—Juvenile literature.
Classification: LCC PL1125.E6 (ebook) | LCC PL1125.E6 .P74 2019 (print) | DDC 495.183/421—dc23

LC record available at https://lccn.loc.gov/2018059334

Manufactured in the United States of America
1-45828-42705-3/15/2019